TO:

_____

FROM:

_____

DATE:

_____

Published by Christian Art Publishers
PO Box 1599, Vereeniging, 1930, RSA

© 2016
First edition 2016

Designed by Christian Art Publishers

Images used under license from Shutterstock.com

Printed in China

ISBN 978-1-4321-1595-1

16 17 18 19 20 21 22 23 24 25 – 12 11 10 9 8 7 6 5 4 3

365 PROMISES
FROM
GOD'S WORD
IN
COLOR

CHRISTIAN ART
PUBLISHERS

1

Glory in His holy name; let the hearts
of those who seek the Lord rejoice.

~ Psalm 105:3 NIV

2

This is the day that the Lord has made;
let us rejoice and be glad in it.

~ Psalm 118:24 ESV

3

Those who sow with tears
will reap with songs of joy.

~ Psalm 126:5 NIV

4

Those who love Your instructions
have great peace and do not stumble.

~ Psalm 119:165 NLT

5

"Peace I leave with you; My peace
I give you. I do not give to you as
the world gives. Do not let your hearts
be troubled and do not be afraid."

~ John 14:27 NIV

6

May the LORD of peace Himself give you
His peace at all times and in every situation.
The LORD be with you all.

~ 2 Thessalonians 3:16 NLT

7

To each one of us grace has been
given as Christ apportioned it.

~ Ephesians 4:7 NIV

8

"My grace is sufficient for you, for My
power is made perfect in weakness."

~ 2 Corinthians 12:9 ESV

9

Let us then approach God's throne of
grace with confidence, so that we may
receive mercy and find grace to help us
in our time of need.

~ Hebrews 4:16 NIV

His grace is sufficient

10

We live by faith, not by sight.

~ 2 Corinthians 5:7 NIV

11

Jesus said, "All things are possible
for one who believes."

~ Mark 9:23 ESV

12

We fix our eyes not on what is seen,
but on what is unseen, since what
is seen is temporary, but what
is unseen is eternal.

~ 2 Corinthians 4:18 NIV

13

We have this hope as an anchor
for the soul, firm and secure.

~ Hebrews 6:19 NIV

14

Joyful are those whose hope is
in the LORD their God.

~ Psalm 146:5 NLT

15

Be strong and take heart,
all you who hope in the LORD.

~ Psalm 31:24 NIV

16

For God so loved the world that He gave
His one and only Son, that whoever
believes in Him shall not perish
but have eternal life.

~ John 3:16 NIV

17

"I lavish unfailing love for a thousand
generations to those who love Me
and obey My commands."

~ Deuteronomy 5:10 NLT

18

"I have loved you with an
everlasting love; I have drawn you
with unfailing kindness."

~ Jeremiah 31:3 NIV

Unfailing love

19

Shout praises to the LORD!
Our God is kind, and it is right
and good to sing praises to Him.

~ Psalm 147:1 CEV

20

The LORD is righteous in everything He
does; He is filled with kindness.

~ Psalm 145:17 NLT

21

Our LORD is kind. He is faithful
and caring, and He saves us.

~ Psalm 40:10 CEV

22

God has surely listened
and has heard my prayer.

~ Psalm 66:19 NIV

23

"I will answer them before they even
call to Me. While they are still talking
about their needs, I will go ahead
and answer their prayers!"

~ Isaiah 65:24 NLT

24

"Then you will call upon Me and go
and pray to Me, and I will listen to you.
And you will seek Me and find Me, when
you search for Me with all your heart."

~ Jeremiah 29:12-13 NKJV

25

The Father is a merciful God,
who always gives us comfort. He
comforts us when we are in trouble,
so that we can share that same
comfort with others in trouble.

~ 2 Corinthians 1:3-4 CEV

26

"As a mother comforts her child,
so will I comfort you."

~ Isaiah 66:13 NIV

27

The LORD will bring comfort.

~ Isaiah 51:3 CEV

28

The LORD will protect you and
keep you safe from all dangers.
The LORD will protect you now
and always wherever you go.

~ Psalm 121:7-8 CEV

29

The name of the LORD is
a fortified tower; the righteous
run to it and are safe.

~ Proverbs 18:10 NIV

30

The LORD is my fortress, protecting
me from danger, so why
should I tremble?

~ Psalm 27:1 NLT

31

God will meet all your needs
according to the riches of
His glory in Christ Jesus.

~ Philippians 4:19 NIV

32

"Your Father knows what you need
before you ask Him."

~ Matthew 6:8 ESV

33

The Lord is my shepherd,
I lack nothing. He makes me
lie down in green pastures,
He leads me beside quiet waters.

~ Psalm 23:1-2 NIV

34

The Lord is gracious and
righteous; our God
is full of compassion.

~ Psalm 116:5 NIV

35

The Lord your God is merciful and
compassionate, slow to get angry
and filled with unfailing love.

~ Joel 2:13 NLT

36

The Lord is compassionate and merciful.

~ James 5:11 ESV

37

Give thanks to the Lord and proclaim
His greatness. Let the whole world
know what He has done.

~ Psalm 105:1 NLT

38

Thanks be to God, who in Christ always leads us in triumphal procession, and through us spreads the fragrance of the knowledge of Him everywhere.

~ 2 Corinthians 2:14 ESV

39

You made all the delicate, inner parts of my body and knit me together in my mother's womb. Thank You for making me so wonderfully complex! Your workmanship is marvelous – how well I know it.

~ Psalm 139:13-14 NLT

40

"I know the plans I have for you,"
declares the LORD, "plans to prosper
you and not to harm you, plans to
give you hope and a future."

~ Jeremiah 29:11 NIV

41

We are God's masterpiece. He has
created us anew in Christ Jesus,
so we can do the good things
He planned for us long ago.

~ Ephesians 2:10 NLT

42

"Before I formed you in the womb
I knew you, and before you were
born I consecrated you; I appointed
you a prophet to the nations."

~ Jeremiah 1:4-5 ESV

43

The wisdom that comes from heaven
is first of all pure; then peace-loving,
considerate, submissive, full of mercy
and good fruit, impartial and sincere.

~ James 3:17 NIV

44

If any of you lacks wisdom,
let him ask God, who gives
generously to all without reproach.

~ James 1:5 ESV

45

The LORD's teachings last forever, and
they give wisdom to ordinary people.

~ Psalm 19:7 CEV

46

The LORD blesses the home of the upright.

~ Proverbs 3:33 NLT

47

May you be blessed by the LORD,
the Maker of heaven and earth.

~ Psalm 115:15 NIV

48

The LORD will indeed give what is good,
and our land will yield its harvest.

~ Psalm 85:12 NIV

The Lord gives what is good

49

Blessed are those who trust in
the LORD and have made the LORD
their hope and confidence.

~ Jeremiah 17:7 NLT

50

In the fear of the LORD there is
strong confidence, and His children
will have a place of refuge.

~ Proverbs 14:26 NKJV

51

We have placed our
confidence in Him, and He
will continue to rescue us.

~ 2 Corinthians 1:10 NLT

52

The LORD gives His people strength.
The LORD blesses them with peace.

~ *Psalm 29:11 NLT*

53

God is our refuge and strength,
an ever-present help in trouble.

~ *Psalm 46:1 NIV*

54

The Sovereign LORD is my strength!
He makes me as surefooted as a deer,
able to tread upon the heights.

~ *Habakkuk 3:19 NLT*

55

Our God is a God of salvation.

~ Psalm 68:20 ESV

56

The LORD lives! Praise to my Rock!
May the God of my salvation be exalted!

~ Psalm 18:46 NLT

57

On God rests my salvation.

~ Psalm 62:7 ESV

58

The LORD's promises are pure,
like silver refined in a furnace,
purified seven times over.

~ Psalm 12:6 NLT

59

God always keeps His promises.

~ Numbers 23:19 CEV

60

The heavens praise Your wonders,
LORD, Your faithfulness too, in the
assembly of the holy ones.

~ Psalm 89:5 NIV

61

The LORD will guide you always; He will satisfy
your needs in a sun-scorched land and will
strengthen your frame. You will be like a well-watered
garden, like a spring whose waters never fail.

~ Isaiah 58:11 NIV

62

The LORD says, "I will guide you along
the best pathway for your life. I will
advise you and watch over you."

~ Psalm 32:8-9 NLT

63

Without guidance from God
law and order disappear, but God
blesses everyone who obeys His Law.

~ Proverbs 29:18 CEV

64

"Where two or three are gathered
together in My name, I am there
in the midst of them."

~ Matthew 18:20 NKJV

65

"Anyone who loves Me will obey
My teaching. My Father will love
them, and We will come to them
and make Our home with them."

~ John 14:23 NIV

66

God is with those who obey Him.

~ Psalm 14:5 NLT

67

Give thanks to the LORD, for He is good;
His love endures forever.

~ *Psalm 107:1 NIV*

68

The LORD is good to everyone. He showers
compassion on all His creation. All of Your
works will thank You, LORD, and Your faithful
followers will praise You.

~ *Psalm 145:9-10 NLT*

69

The LORD bestows favor and honor;
no good thing does He withhold
from those whose walk is blameless.

~ *Psalm 84:11 NIV*

70

"I know you by name, and you
have also found favor in My sight."

~ Exodus 33:12 ESV

71

Surely, LORD, You bless the righteous;
You surround them with Your
favor as with a shield.

~ Psalm 5:12 NIV

72

Sing praises to God and to His name!
Sing loud praises to Him who rides
the clouds. His name is the LORD –
rejoice in His presence!

~ Psalm 68:4 NLT

73

Praise be to the LORD God, the God of Israel,
who alone does marvelous deeds. Praise be
to His glorious name forever; may the
whole earth be filled with His glory.

~ Psalm 72:18-19 NIV

74

I will praise the LORD according
to His righteousness, and
will sing praise to the name
of the LORD Most High.

~ Psalm 7:17 NKJV

75

"Rejoice because your names
are written in heaven."

~ Luke 10:20 NKJV

76

"Be happy! Yes, leap for joy! For a
great reward awaits you in heaven."

~ Luke 6:23 NLT

77

In Him our hearts rejoice,
for we trust in His holy name.

~ Psalm 33:21 NIV

78

To us a Child is born. And He will
be called Wonderful Counselor,
Mighty God, Everlasting Father,
Prince of Peace.

~ Isaiah 9:6 NIV

79

The LORD said, "My presence will go with you,
and I will give you rest."

~ Exodus 33:14 ESV

80

"Come to Me, all you who are weary and burdened,
and I will give you rest. Take My yoke upon you
and learn from Me, for I am gentle and humble
in heart, and you will find rest for your souls."

~ Matthew 11:28-29 NIV

81

God saved you by His grace when you believed.
And you can't take credit for this;
it is a gift from God.

~ Ephesians 2:8 NLT

82

God is able to make all grace abound to
you, so that having all sufficiency in all
things at all times, you may abound
in every good work.

~ 2 Corinthians 9:8 ESV

83

Sin is no longer your master, for you
no longer live under the requirements
of the law. Instead, you live under the
freedom of God's grace.

~ Romans 6:14 NLT

84

"I tell you the truth, if you had faith even as
small as a mustard seed, you could say to this
mountain, 'Move from here to there,' and it
would move. Nothing would be impossible."

~ Matthew 17:20 NLT

85

Be on your guard; stand firm in the
faith; be courageous; be strong.

~ 1 Corinthians 16:13 NIV

86

Now faith is the substance
of things hoped for, the evidence
of things not seen.

~ Hebrews 11:1 NKJV

87

Hope in the LORD! For with the LORD
there is steadfast love, and with Him
is plentiful redemption.

~ Psalm 130:7 ESV

Stand firm in faith

88

The LORD is good to those whose hope is in Him.

~ Lamentations 3:25 NIV

89

Rejoice in hope, be patient in tribulation,
be constant in prayer.

~ Romans 12:12 ESV

90

See how very much our Father loves us, for He
calls us His children, and that is what we are!

~ 1 John 3:1 NLT

91

I am like an olive tree growing in
God's house, and I can count on
His love forever and ever.

~ Psalm 52:8 CEV

92

This is real love – not that we loved
God, but that He loved us and
sent His Son as a sacrifice to
take away our sins.

~ 1 John 4:10 NLT

93

LORD, You have always been
patient and kind.

~ Psalm 25:6 CEV

94

God raised us up with Christ and seated us with Him in
the heavenly realms in Christ Jesus, in order that in the
coming ages He might show the incomparable riches of
His grace, expressed in His kindness to us in Christ Jesus.

~ Ephesians 2:6-7 NIV

95

The prayer of a righteous person
is powerful and effective.

~ James 5:16 NIV

96

"Whatever you ask in My name,
that I will do."

~ John 14:13 NKJV

97

The eyes of the Lord are on
the righteous and His ears
are attentive to their prayer.

~ 1 Peter 3:12 NIV

98

The Lord comforts His people
and will have compassion
on His afflicted ones.

~ Isaiah 49:13 NIV

99

As we share abundantly in Christ's
sufferings, so through Christ we
share abundantly in comfort too.

~ 2 Corinthians 1:5 ESV

100

"I will comfort those who mourn,"
says the LORD.

~ Isaiah 57:18-19 NLT

101

The LORD is faithful, and He will strengthen you
and protect you from the evil one.

~ 2 Thessalonians 3:3 NIV

102

You are my fortress, my place of safety;
You are my God, and I trust You.

~ Psalm 91:2 CEV

103

"Be strong and courageous.
Do not be frightened, and do not
be dismayed, for the LORD your God
is with you wherever you go."

~ Joshua 1:9 ESV

104

He provides food for those
who fear Him; He remembers
His covenant forever.

~ Psalm 111:5 ESV

105

"Seek the Kingdom of God
above all else, and He will give you
everything you need."

~ Luke 12:31 NLT

106

The LORD your God is a merciful
God. He will not leave you.

~ *Deuteronomy 4:31 ESV*

107

Praise be to the LORD, for
He has heard my cry for mercy.

~ *Psalm 28:6 NIV*

108

The LORD your God is gracious
and merciful and will not turn
away His face from you.

~ *2 Chronicles 30:9 ESV*

109

Thanks be to God for His
indescribable gift!

~ *2 Corinthians 9:15 NKJV*

110

Enter His gates with thanksgiving
and His courts with praise; give
thanks to Him and praise His name.

~ *Psalm 100:4 NIV*

111

Thank God! He gives us victory
over sin and death through our
Lord Jesus Christ.

~ *1 Corinthians 15:57 NLT*

112

Even before He made the world, God loved us and chose us in Christ to be holy and without fault in His eyes. God decided in advance to adopt us into His own family by bringing us to Himself through Jesus Christ.

~ Ephesians 1:4-5 NLT

113

Many are the plans in a person's heart,
but it is the Lord's purpose that prevails.

~ Proverbs 19:21 NIV

114

God gives wisdom to the wise
and knowledge to the discerning.

~ Daniel 2:21 NIV

Wisdom from God

115

With God are wisdom and might;
He has counsel and understanding.

~ Job 12:13 ESV

116

God alone understands the way to wisdom;
He knows where it can be found.

~ Job 28:23 NLT

117

The LORD has been mindful of us;
He will bless us. He will bless those who
fear the LORD, both small and great.

~ Psalm 115:12-13 NKJV

118

When You open Your hand, You satisfy the hunger
and thirst of every living thing. The Lord is righteous
in everything He does; He is filled with kindness.

~ Psalm 145:16-17 NLT

119

The blessing of the LORD brings wealth,
without painful toil for it.

~ Proverbs 10:22 NIV

120

It is better to trust in the LORD
than to put confidence in man.

~ Psalm 118:8 NKJV

121

We can say with confidence,
"The LORD is my helper,
so I will have no fear."

~ Hebrews 13:6 NLT

122

Such is the confidence that we have through
Christ toward God. Not that we are sufficient
in ourselves to claim anything as coming from us,
but our sufficiency is from God.

~ 2 Corinthians 3:4-5 ESV

123

The LORD is my strength and my shield; in Him my
heart trusts, and I am helped; my heart exults,
and with my song I give thanks to Him.

~ Psalm 28:7 ESV

In Him my heart trusts

124

Be strong in the Lord and
in His mighty power.

~ Ephesians 6:10 NIV

125

In Your strength I can crush an army;
with my God I can scale any wall.

~ Psalm 18:29 NLT

126

We are surrounded by the walls
of God's salvation.

~ Isaiah 26:1 NLT

127

There is no other name under heaven
by which we must be saved.

~ Acts 4:12 NKJV

128

The salvation of the righteous comes from the LORD.

~ Psalm 37:39 NIV

129

The LORD will cover you with His feathers.
He will shelter you with His wings. His faithful
promises are your armor and protection.

~ Psalm 91:4 NLT

130

Know therefore that the LORD your God is God;
He is the faithful God, keeping His covenant of love
to a thousand generations of those who love Him
and keep His commandments.

~ Deuteronomy 7:9 NIV

131

The LORD always keeps His promises;
He is gracious in all He does.

~ Psalm 145:13 NLT

132

The Lamb in the midst of the throne
will be their shepherd, and He will
guide them to springs of living water.

~ Revelation 7:17 ESV

133

Everything in the Scriptures is God's
Word. All of it is useful for teaching
and helping people and for correcting
them and showing them how to live.

~ 2 Timothy 3:16 CEV

134

The Lord's word is a lamp to my feet
and a light to my path.

~ Psalm 119:105 ESV

135

The Lord your God is with you, the Mighty Warrior
who saves. He will take great delight in you;
in His love He will no longer rebuke you,
but will rejoice over you with singing.

~ Zephaniah 3:17 NIV

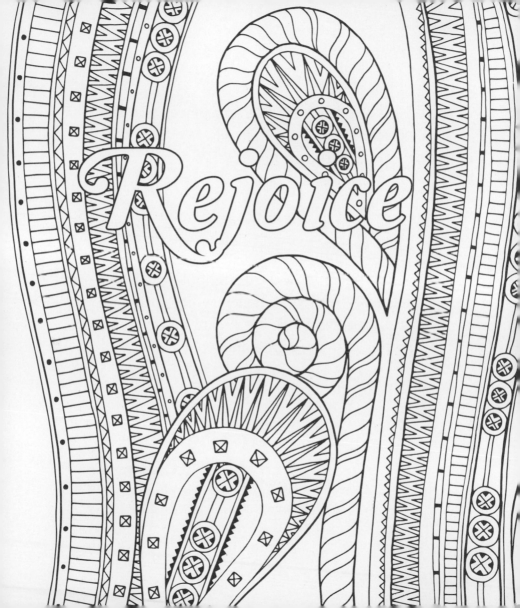

136

The eyes of the LORD are in every place,
keeping watch on the evil
and the good.

~ Proverbs 15:3 NKJV

137

"I will be your God throughout your
lifetime – until your hair is white with
age. I made you and I will care for you.
I will carry you along and save you."

~ Isaiah 46:4 NLT

138

Praise the LORD! Give thanks
to the LORD, for He is good!
His faithful love endures forever.

~ Psalm 106:1 NLT

139

His divine power has given us everything we need
for a godly life through our knowledge of Him
who called us by His own glory and goodness.

~ 2 Peter 1:3 NIV

140

For the LORD God is a sun and shield;
the LORD will give grace and glory;
no good thing will He withhold
from those who walk uprightly.

~ Psalm 84:11 NKJV

141

"Whoever finds Me finds life and
receives favor from the LORD."

~ Proverbs 8:35 NLT

142

Glory to God in the highest heaven,
and on earth peace to those
on whom His favor rests.

~ Luke 2:14 NIV

143

You have granted me life and favor,
and Your care has preserved my spirit.

~ Job 10:12 NKJV

144

Let them praise the name of the LORD,
for His name alone is exalted; His
majesty is above earth and heaven.

~ Psalm 148:13 ESV

145

Praise the LORD! Sing to the LORD
a new song. Sing His praises in
the assembly of the faithful.

~ Psalm 149:1 NLT

146

Declare His glory among the nations,
His wonders among all peoples. For the
LORD is great and greatly to be praised;
He is also to be feared above all gods.

~ 1 Chronicles 16:24-25 NKJV

147

The joy of the LORD is your strength.

~ Nehemiah 8:10 NKJV

148

When Your words came, I ate them;
they were my joy and my heart's delight.

~ Jeremiah 15:16 NIV

149

The LORD will make you successful
in everything you do. You will
be completely happy.

~ Deuteronomy 16:15 CEV

150

"In Me you may have peace.
In the world you will have tribulation;
but be of good cheer, I have
overcome the world."

~ John 16:33 NKJV

151

The LORD your God will give you rest.

~ Deuteronomy 12:10 NIV

152

"I Myself will tend My sheep and
give them a place to lie down in peace,"
says the Sovereign LORD.

~ Ezekiel 34:15 NLT

153

From His abundance we have all received
one gracious blessing after another.

~ John 1:16 NLT

One blessing
after another

154

The Lord is compassionate
and gracious, slow to anger,
abounding in love.

~ Psalm 103:8 NIV

155

We praise God for the glorious
grace He has poured out on us
who belong to His dear Son.

~ Ephesians 1:6 NLT

156

For in the gospel the righteousness of God
is revealed – a righteousness that is by
faith from first to last, just as it is written:
"The righteous will live by faith."

~ Romans 1:17 NIV

157

Because of Christ and our faith in Him,
we can now come boldly and
confidently into God's presence.

~ Ephesians 3:12 NLT

158

In all circumstances take up the shield
of faith, with which you can extinguish
all the flaming darts of the evil one.

~ Ephesians 6:16 ESV

159

May the God of hope fill you with
all joy and peace as you trust in Him,
so that you may overflow with hope
by the power of the Holy Spirit.

~ Romans 15:13 NIV

160

The LORD renews our hopes
and heals our bodies.

~ Psalm 147:3 CEV

161

"Know that I am the LORD;
those who hope in Me
will not be disappointed."

~ Isaiah 49:23 NIV

162

This is how we know what love is:
Jesus Christ laid down His life for
us. And we ought to lay down our
lives for our brothers and sisters.

~ 1 John 3:16 NIV

163

God showed how much He loved us by sending
His one and only Son into the world so that we
might have eternal life through Him.

~ 1 John 4:9 NLT

164

Because of the LORD's great love we are not
consumed, for His compassions never fail. They
are new every morning; great is Your faithfulness.

~ Lamentations 3:22-23 NIV

165

Christ has also introduced us to God's
undeserved kindness on which we take our stand.

~ Romans 5:2 CEV

166

When God our Savior revealed His
kindness and love, He saved us, not
because of the righteous things we
had done, but because of His mercy.

~ Titus 3:4-5 NLT

167

The LORD loves justice and fairness,
and He is kind to everyone
everywhere on earth.

~ Psalm 33:5 CEV

168

"If you abide in Me, and My words
abide in you, ask whatever you wish,
and it will be done for you."

~ John 15:7 ESV

169

"Whatever you ask for in prayer,
believe that you have received it,
and it will be yours."

~ Mark 11:24 NIV

170

"Ask, and it will be given to you;
seek, and you will find; knock,
and it will be opened to you."

~ Matthew 7:7 NKJV

171

He heals the brokenhearted
and binds up their wounds.

~ Psalm 147:3 NIV

172

Let Your unfailing love comfort me,
just as You promised me.

~ Psalm 119:76 NLT

173

"Blessed are those who mourn,
for they will be comforted."

~ Matthew 5:4 NIV

174

You can be sure that the LORD
will protect you from harm.

~ Proverbs 3:26 CEV

The Lord will protect you

175

The LORD your God will personally go ahead of
you. He will neither fail you nor abandon you.

~ Deuteronomy 31:6 NLT

176

"Fear not, for I am with you; be not dismayed,
for I am your God; I will strengthen you,
I will help you, I will uphold you."

~ Isaiah 41:10 ESV

177

God is the One who provides seed for the farmer
and then bread to eat. In the same way, He will
provide and increase your resources and then
produce a great harvest of generosity in you.

~ 2 Corinthians 9:10 NLT

178

"Give, and it will be given to you.
A good measure, pressed down, shaken
together and running over, will be poured
into your lap. For with the measure you
use, it will be measured to you."

~ Luke 6:38 NIV

179

"Therefore do not be anxious, saying,
'What shall we eat?' or 'What shall
we drink?' or 'What shall we wear?'
For the Gentiles seek after all these
things, and your heavenly Father
knows that you need them all."

~ Matthew 6:31-32 ESV

180

The LORD God is famous for His
wonderful deeds, and He is
kind and merciful.

~ Psalm 111:4 CEV

181

Goodness and mercy shall
follow me all the days of my life,
and I shall dwell in the house
of the LORD forever.

~ Psalm 23:6 ESV

182

In panic I cried out, "I am cut off
from the LORD!" But You heard
my cry for mercy and answered
my call for help.

~ Psalm 31:22 NLT

183

Oh give thanks to the LORD;
call upon His name; make known
His deeds among the peoples!

~ 1 Chronicles 16:8 ESV

184

We give thanks to You, O God,
we give thanks! For Your wondrous
works declare that Your name is near.

~ Psalm 75:1 NKJV

185

May you be filled with joy,
always thanking the Father.

~ Colossians 1:11-12 NLT

May you be
filled with joy

186

The LORD says, "I will guide you along
the best pathway for your life. I will
advise you and watch over you."

~ Psalm 32:8 NLT

187

The plans of the LORD stand firm
forever, the purposes of His heart
through all generations.

~ Psalm 33:11 NIV

188

"Call to Me, and I will answer you,
and show you great and mighty
things, which you do not know."

~ Jeremiah 33:3 NKJV

189

Blessed are those who find wisdom,
those who gain understanding.

~ Proverbs 3:13 NIV

190

Wisdom is like honey for your life –
if you find it, your future is bright.

~ Proverbs 24:14 CEV

191

Do not forsake wisdom, and she will protect you;
love her, and she will watch over you.

~ Proverbs 4:6 NIV

192

Blessed are those whose ways are blameless,
who walk according to the law of the LORD.

~ Psalm 119:1 NIV

193

The LORD will send rain at the proper time
from His rich treasury in the heavens
and will bless all the work you do.

~ Deuteronomy 28:12 NLT

194

LORD, You alone are my inheritance, my cup of blessing.
You guard all that is mine. The land You have given me
is a pleasant land. What a wonderful inheritance!

~ Psalm 16:5-6 NLT

195

You have been my hope, Sovereign
LORD, my confidence since my youth.

~ Psalm 71:5 NIV

196

By awesome deeds in righteousness You
will answer us, O God of our salvation,
You who are the confidence of all the
ends of the earth, and of the far-off seas.

~ Psalm 65:5 NKJV

197

The LORD will be your confidence and
will keep your foot from being caught.

~ Proverbs 3:26 ESV

198

The LORD is my strength and my song; He has given me victory. This is my God, and I will praise Him – my father's God, and I will exalt Him!

~ Exodus 15:2 NLT

199

"In repentance and rest is your salvation, in quietness and trust is your strength."

~ Isaiah 30:15 NIV

200

Turn to God. Then times of refreshment will come from the presence of the Lord.

~ Acts 3:19-20 NLT

The Lord is my strength

201

"Let all the world look to
Me for salvation! For I am God;
there is no other."

~ Isaiah 45:22 NLT

202

The LORD lives, and blessed be
my Rock, and exalted be my God,
the Rock of my salvation.

~ 2 Samuel 22:47 ESV

203

It is good to wait quietly for
the salvation of the LORD.

~ Lamentations 3:26 NIV

204

If we are faithless, He remains
faithful; He cannot deny Himself.

~ 2 Timothy 2:13 NKJV

205

The Scriptures tell us,
"Anyone who trusts in Him
will never be disgraced."

~ Romans 10:11 NLT

206

Sovereign LORD, You are God!
Your covenant is trustworthy.

~ 2 Samuel 7:28 NIV

207

Don't just listen to God's Word.
You must do what it says.

~ James 1:22 NLT

208

The LORD our God will lead the way.

~ Deuteronomy 1:30 CEV

209

God is with us; He is our leader.

~ 2 Chronicles 13:12 NIV

The Lord will lead us

210

"Surely I am with you always,
to the very end of the age."

~ Matthew 28:20 NIV

211

O LORD, You have searched me and known me. You know
my sitting down and my rising up; You understand
my thought afar off. You comprehend my path and my
lying down, and are acquainted with all my ways.

~ Psalm 139:1-3 NKJV

212

"I saw the Lord always before me. Because
He is at my right hand, I will not be shaken."

~ Acts 2:25 NIV

213

You are good, and what You do
is good; teach me Your decrees.

~ Psalm 119:68 NIV

214

For You, O Lord, are good and
forgiving, abounding in steadfast
love to all who call upon You.

~ Psalm 86:5 ESV

215

Good and upright is the LORD;
therefore He instructs sinners in His
ways. He guides the humble in what
is right and teaches them His way.

~ Psalm 25:8-9 NIV

216

A good name is to be chosen rather than great riches, and favor is better than silver or gold.

~ Proverbs 22:1 ESV

217

And I am certain that God,
who began the good work within you,
will continue His work until it is finally
finished on the day when Christ Jesus returns.

~ Philippians 1:6 NLT

218

Let love and faithfulness never leave you;
bind them around your neck, write them on the
tablet of your heart. Then you will win favor and
a good name in the sight of God and man.

~ Proverbs 3:3-4 NIV

219

Let heaven and earth praise Him,
the seas and all that move in them.

~ Psalm 69:34 NIV

220

I will praise the name of God
with a song; I will magnify Him
with thanksgiving.

~ Psalm 69:30 ESV

221

Let everything that has breath
praise the LORD. Praise the LORD.

~ Psalm 150:6 NIV

222

You turned my wailing into dancing; You
removed my sackcloth and clothed me with joy.

~ Psalm 30:11 NIV

223

Those who look to Him for help will
be radiant with joy; no shadow of shame
will darken their faces.

~ Psalm 34:5 NLT

224

The precepts of the LORD are right, giving
joy to the heart. The commands of the LORD
are radiant, giving light to the eyes.

~ Psalm 19:8 NIV

225

The mind governed by the Spirit
is life and peace.

~ Romans 8:6 NIV

226

The peace of God, which surpasses all
understanding, will guard your hearts
and your minds in Christ Jesus.

~ Philippians 4:7 ESV

227

You will keep in perfect peace
those whose minds are steadfast,
because they trust in You.

~ Isaiah 26:3 NIV

228

For the grace of God has appeared,
bringing salvation for all people.

~ Titus 2:11 ESV

229

We are all saved the same way,
by the undeserved grace of the Lord Jesus.

~ Acts 15:11 NLT

230

By the grace of God I am what I am, and His
grace toward me was not in vain. On the contrary,
I worked harder than any of them, though it was
not I, but the grace of God that is with me.

~ 1 Corinthians 15:10 ESV

231

Trust in the LORD with all your heart;
do not depend on your own understanding.
Seek His will in all you do, and
He will show you which path to take.

~ Proverbs 3:5-6 NLT

232

Faith comes from hearing the message,
and the message is heard through
the word about Christ.

~ Romans 10:17 NIV

Trust
in the Lord.

233

Without faith it is impossible to please Him,
for he who comes to God must believe that
He is, and that He is a rewarder of those
who diligently seek Him.

~ Hebrews 11:6 NKJV

234

Hope deferred makes the heart sick,
but a dream fulfilled is a tree of life.

~ Proverbs 13:12 NLT

235

No one who hopes in You, LORD,
will ever be put to shame.

~ Psalm 25:3 NIV

236

The hope of the righteous
will be gladness.

~ Proverbs 10:28 NKJV

237

Give thanks to the God of gods.
His love endures forever.

~ Psalm 136:2 NIV

238

"I have loved you even as the Father
has loved Me. Remain in My love."

~ John 15:9 NLT

239

"Greater love has no one than this:
to lay down one's life for one's friends."

~ John 15:13 NIV

240

Jesus Christ alone brought God's
gift of kindness to many people.

~ Romans 5:15 CEV

241

Tell the Lord how thankful
you are, because He is kind
and always merciful.

~ Psalm 118:1 CEV

242

Praise the name of the LORD!
He is kind and good.

~ Psalm 135:3 CEV

243

The LORD is near to all who call on
Him, to all who call on Him in truth.
He fulfills the desire of those
who fear Him.

~ Psalm 145:18-19 ESV

244

Pray in the Spirit on all occasions with
all kinds of prayers and requests. With
this in mind, be alert and always keep
on praying for all the Lord's people.

~ Ephesians 6:18 NIV

245

"Whatever things you ask in prayer,
believing, you will receive."

~ Matthew 21:22 NKJV

246

"I, yes I, am the one who comforts you.
So why are you afraid?"

~ Isaiah 51:12 NLT

247

Though I walk in the midst of trouble,
You preserve my life; You stretch out Your
hand against the wrath of my enemies,
and Your right hand delivers me.

~ Psalm 138:7 ESV

248

The LORD upholds all who fall,
and raises up all who are bowed down.

~ Psalm 145:14 NKJV

249

"I am the LORD your God who takes
hold of your right hand and says to
you, Do not fear; I will help you."

~ Isaiah 41:13 NIV

250

No one is like the LORD! You protect
the helpless from those in power;
You save the poor and needy from
those who hurt them.

~ Psalm 35:10 CEV

251

Even when I walk through the darkest valley, I will
not be afraid, for You, LORD, are close beside me.
Your rod and Your staff protect and comfort me.

~ Psalm 23:4 NLT

252

"Seek the Kingdom of God above all else,
and live righteously, and He will
give you everything you need."

~ Matthew 6:33 NLT

253

"Consider the ravens, for they neither sow nor
reap, which have neither storehouse nor barn;
and God feeds them. Of how much more
value are you than the birds?"

~ Luke 12:24 NKJV

254

"I will open the windows of heaven
for you. I will pour out a blessing so
great you won't have enough room to
take it in. Try it! Put Me to the test!"

~ Malachi 3:10 NLT

255

Let every true worshiper of the LORD
shout, "God is always merciful!"

~ Psalm 118:4 CEV

256

The Lord our God
is merciful and forgiving.

~ Daniel 9:9 NLT

257

God was merciful! We were dead because of our sins, but God loved us so much that He made us alive with Christ, and God's wonderful kindness is what saves you.

~ Ephesians 2:4 CEV

258

Sing and make music from your heart to the Lord, always giving thanks to God the Father for everything, in the name of our Lord Jesus Christ.

~ Ephesians 5:19-20 NIV

259

Whatever you do, in word or deed, do everything in the name of the Lord Jesus, giving thanks to God the Father through Him.

~ Colossians 3:17 ESV

260

Be thankful in all circumstances,
for this is God's will for you
who belong to Christ Jesus.

~ 1 Thessalonians 5:18 NLT

261

I know, LORD, that our lives are
not our own. We are not able
to plan our own course.

~ Jeremiah 10:23 NLT

262

In their hearts humans plan
their course, but the LORD
establishes their steps.

~ Proverbs 16:9 NIV

263

I am trusting You, O LORD,
saying, "You are my God!"
My future is in Your hands.

~ Psalm 31:14-15 NLT

264

Instruct the wise and they will
be wiser still; teach the righteous
and they will add to their learning.

~ Proverbs 9:9 NIV

265

Listen to counsel and receive
instruction, that you may be
wise in your latter days.

~ Proverbs 19:20 NKJV

You are my God

266

By wisdom a house is built, and
by understanding it is established;
by knowledge the rooms are filled
with all precious and pleasant riches.

~ Proverbs 24:3-4 ESV

267

When God blesses His people,
their city prospers.

~ Proverbs 11:11 CEV

268

If you know what you're doing,
you will prosper. God blesses
everyone who trusts Him.

~ Proverbs 16:20 CEV

269

Because of Christ there are blessings
that cannot be measured.

~ Ephesians 3:8 CEV

270

Now this is the confidence that we
have in Him, that if we ask anything
according to His will, He hears us.

~ 1 John 5:14 NKJV

271

Oh, the joys of those who trust the
LORD, who have no confidence in the
proud or in those who worship idols.

~ Psalm 40:4 NLT

272

The fruit of that righteousness
will be peace; its effect will be
quietness and confidence forever.

~ Isaiah 32:17 NIV

273

"I will search for My lost ones,
and I will bring them safely home
again. I will bandage the injured
and strengthen the weak."

~ Ezekiel 34:16 NLT

274

God is my strength and power, and He makes my way perfect. He makes my feet like the feet of deer, and sets me on my high places.

~ 2 Samuel 22:33-34 NKJV

275

The LORD is my strength and my song;
He has given me victory.

~ Psalm 118:14 NLT

276

Lead me in Your truth and teach me,
for You are the God of my salvation.

~ Psalm 25:5 ESV

277

"It is I, the LORD, announcing your
salvation! It is I, the LORD, who has
the power to save!"

~ Isaiah 63:1 NLT

278

Why are you cast down, O my soul,
and why are you in turmoil within me?
Hope in God; for I shall again praise
Him, my salvation and my God.

~ Psalm 42:11 ESV

279

Your decrees are very trustworthy;
holiness befits Your house,
O LORD, forevermore.

~ Psalm 93:5 ESV

280

God is faithful, who has called
you into fellowship with His Son,
Jesus Christ our Lord.

~ 1 Corinthians 1:9 NIV

281

Steadfast love will be built up forever;
in the heavens You will establish
Your faithfulness.

~ Psalm 89:2 ESV

282

"I am the LORD your God,
who teaches you to profit, who
leads you in the way you should go."

~ Isaiah 48:17 ESV

283

The LORD God of Israel will
lead and protect you.

~ Isaiah 52:12 CEV

284

The LORD Himself will guide you.

~ Micah 2:13 NLT

285

"No, I will not abandon you as
orphans – I will come to you."

~ John 14:18 NLT

The Lord will guide you

286

If I go up to the heavens, You are there;
if I make my bed in the depths, You are
there. If I rise on the wings of the dawn,
if I settle on the far side of the sea,
even there Your hand will guide me,
Your right hand will hold me fast.

~ Psalm 139:8-10 NIV

287

"I am with you, and I will protect you
wherever you go. I will not leave
you until I have finished giving you
everything I have promised you."

~ Genesis 28:15 NLT

288

Every good gift and every perfect gift is from above, and comes down from the Father of lights, with whom there is no variation or shadow of turning.

~ James 1:17 NKJV

289

The LORD is good, a strong refuge when trouble comes. He is close to those who trust in Him.

~ Nahum 1:7 NLT

290

Restore us, O LORD God of hosts; cause Your face to shine, and we shall be saved!

~ Psalm 80:19 NKJV

291

Let the favor of the Lord our God
be upon us, and establish the work
of our hands upon us; yes, establish
the work of our hands!

~ Psalm 90:17 ESV

292

Remember me, O LORD, with the
favor You have toward Your people.

~ Psalm 106:4 NKJV

293

With all my heart I will praise You,
O Lord my God. I will give glory
to Your name forever, for Your
love for me is very great.

~ Psalm 86:12-13 NLT

294

Sing praises to God, sing praises! Sing praises to our King, sing praises! For God is the King of all the earth; sing praises with a psalm!

~ Psalm 47:6-7 ESV

295

Let all that I am praise the LORD. O LORD my God, how great You are! You are robed with honor and majesty. You are dressed in a robe of light.

~ Psalm 104:1-2 NLT

296

Honor and majesty are before Him; strength and gladness are in His place.

~ 1 Chronicles 16:27 NKJV

Let all
that I am
praise
the *Lord*

297

The LORD has done great things
for us, and we are filled with joy.

~ Psalm 126:3 NIV

298

Let the heavens be glad,
and let the earth rejoice,
and let them say among the
nations, "The LORD reigns!"

~ 1 Chronicles 16:31 ESV

299

God is not a God of confusion
but of peace.

~ 1 Corinthians 14:33 ESV

300

He was wounded for our transgressions,
He was bruised for our iniquities; the
chastisement for our peace was upon Him,
and by His stripes we are healed.

~ Isaiah 53:5 NKJV

301

The kingdom of God is not a
matter of eating and drinking
but of righteousness and peace
and joy in the Holy Spirit.

~ Romans 14:17 ESV

302

You know the generous grace of our Lord
Jesus Christ. Though He was rich, yet for
your sakes He became poor, so that by
His poverty He could make you rich.

~ 2 Corinthians 8:9 NLT

303

The God of all grace, who called you to His
eternal glory in Christ, after you have suffered
a little while, will Himself restore you and
make you strong, firm and steadfast.

~ 1 Peter 5:10 NIV

304

Because of His grace He declared us
righteous and gave us confidence that
we will inherit eternal life.

~ Titus 3:7 NLT

305

I can do everything through Christ,
who gives me strength.

~ Philippians 4:13 NLT

306

Everyone who believes that Jesus is the Christ has been born of God, and everyone who loves the Father loves whoever has been born of Him.

~ 1 John 5:1 ESV

307

"Anyone who believes and is baptized will be saved. But anyone who refuses to believe will be condemned."

~ Mark 16:16 NLT

308

Those who hope in the LORD will renew their strength. They will soar on wings like eagles; they will run and not grow weary, they will walk and not be faint.

~ Isaiah 40:31 NIV

309

Let us hold fast the confession of our hope without wavering, for He who promised is faithful.

~ Hebrews 10:23 ESV

310

We also glory in our sufferings, because we know that suffering produces perseverance; perseverance, character; and character, hope.

~ Romans 5:3-4 NIV

311

Praise the LORD, all nations! Extol Him, all peoples! For great is His steadfast love toward us, and the faithfulness of the LORD endures forever. Praise the LORD!

~ Psalm 117:1-2 ESV

312

It is good to give thanks to the LORD,
to sing praises to Your name, O Most
High; to declare Your steadfast love in the
morning, and Your faithfulness by night,
to the music of the lute and the harp,
to the melody of the lyre.

~ Psalm 92:1-3 ESV

313

The LORD is kind to everyone
who is humble.

~ Proverbs 3:34 CEV

314

God our Father loves us. He is kind and has
given us eternal comfort and a wonderful hope.

~ 2 Thessalonians 2:16 CEV

315

Consider therefore the kindness and sternness of God:
sternness to those who fell, but kindness to you,
provided that you continue in His kindness.

~ Romans 11:22 NIV

316

"When you pray, go into your room,
close the door and pray to your Father,
who is unseen. Then your Father, who sees
what is done in secret, will reward you."

~ Matthew 6:6 NIV

317

"Truly, truly, I say to you, whatever
you ask of the Father in My name,
He will give it to you."

~ John 16:23 ESV

318

Is anyone among you in trouble?
Let them pray. Is anyone happy?
Let them sing songs of praise.

~ James 5:13 NIV

319

Come, let us bow down in worship,
let us kneel before the LORD our Maker;
for He is our God and we are the people
of His pasture, the flock under His care.

~ Psalm 95:6-7 NIV

320

The LORD is close to the brokenhearted;
He rescues those whose spirits are crushed.

~ Psalm 34:18 NLT

321

Though You have made me see troubles, many and
bitter, You will restore my life again; from the depths
of the earth You will again bring me up. You will
increase my honor and comfort me once more.

~ Psalm 71:20-21 NIV

322

It is good for me to be near You, God.
I choose You as my Protector, and I will
tell about Your wonderful deeds.

~ Psalm 73:28 CEV

323

The LORD is on my side; I will not fear.
What can man do to me?

~ Psalm 118:6 ESV

324

God will protect you from harm,
no matter how often trouble may strike.

~ Job 5:19 CEV

325

The lions may grow weak and hungry,
but those who seek the LORD
lack no good thing.

~ Psalm 34:10 NIV

326

"Every moving thing that lives shall be food for you. I have given you all things, even as the green herbs."

~ Genesis 9:3 NKJV

327

You care for the land and water it; You enrich it abundantly. The streams of God are filled with water to provide the people with grain, for so You have ordained it.

~ Psalm 65:9 NIV

328

Great is Your mercy, O LORD;
give me life according to Your rules.

~ Psalm 119:156 ESV

329

All praise to God, the Father of our LORD Jesus
Christ. It is by His great mercy that we
have been born again.

~ 1 Peter 1:3 NLT

330

The LORD waits to be gracious to you,
and therefore He exalts Himself to show mercy
to you. For the LORD is a God of justice;
blessed are all those who wait for Him.

~ Isaiah 30:18 ESV

The Lord is just

331

You are my God, and I will give thanks to You;
You are my God; I will extol You.

~ *Psalm 118:28* ESV

332

Make thankfulness your sacrifice
to God, and keep the vows you
made to the Most High.

~ *Psalm 50:14* NLT

333

"The one who offers thanksgiving as
his sacrifice glorifies Me; to one who
orders his way rightly I will show
the salvation of God!"

~ *Psalm 50:23* ESV

334

"I am God, and there is none like Me. Only I can tell you the future before it even happens."

~ Isaiah 46:9-10 NLT

335

You, LORD God, have done many wonderful things, and You have planned marvelous things for us.

~ Psalm 40:5 CEV

336

God saved us and called us to live a holy life. He did this, not because we deserved it, but because that was His plan from before the beginning of time – to show us His grace through Christ Jesus.

~ 2 Timothy 1:9 NLT

337

The fear of the Lord is the beginning
of wisdom, and knowledge of the
Holy One is understanding.

~ *Proverbs 9:10 NIV*

338

"God blesses those people
who make peace. They will be
called His children."

~ *Matthew 5:9 CEV*

339

Submit to God and be at peace
with Him; in this way prosperity
will come to you.

~ *Job 22:21 NIV*

340

"Blessed are those who hunger and thirst
for righteousness, for they shall be satisfied."

~ Matthew 5:6 ESV

341

Let us who live in the light be clearheaded,
protected by the armor of faith and love,
and wearing as our helmet the
confidence of our salvation.

~ 1 Thessalonians 5:8 NLT

342

Let's come near God with pure hearts
and a confidence that comes from having faith.

~ Hebrews 10:22 CEV

343

Now we have confidence in
a better hope, through which
we draw near to God.

~ Hebrews 7:19 NLT

344

I thank and praise You, God of
my ancestors, for You have given
me wisdom and strength.

~ Daniel 2:23 NLT

345

He gives strength to the weary
and increases the power of the weak.

~ Isaiah 40:29 NIV

346

My health may fail, and my spirit
may grow weak, but God
remains the strength of my heart;
He is mine forever.

~ Psalm 73:26 NLT

347

All the ends of the earth have seen
the salvation of our God.

~ Psalm 98:3 ESV

348

God is my King from long ago;
He brings salvation on the earth.

~ Psalm 74:12 NIV

349

God is my salvation; I will trust, and will
not be afraid; for the LORD GOD
is my strength and my song, and
He has become my salvation.

~ Isaiah 12:2 ESV

350

You remain faithful in every
generation, and the earth You
created will keep standing firm.

~ Psalm 119:90 CEV

351

He is the Maker of heaven and earth,
the sea, and everything in them –
He remains faithful forever.

~ Psalm 146:6 NIV

352

I will sing of the LORD's unfailing
love forever! Young and old will hear
of Your faithfulness.

~ Psalm 89:1 NLT

353

We must keep our eyes on Jesus,
who leads us and makes our faith complete.

~ Hebrews 12:2 CEV

354

You have shown me the way of life,
LORD, and You will fill me with the
joy of Your presence.

~ Acts 2:28 NLT

355

"I am the LORD, and I lead you along the right path.
If you obey Me, we will walk together."

~ Hosea 14:9 CEV

356

For the LORD will not forsake His people,
for His great name's sake, because it has
pleased the LORD to make you His people.

~ 1 Samuel 12:22 NKJV

357

"I will ask the Father, and He
will give you another Advocate, who
will never leave you. He is the Holy Spirit,
who leads into all truth. He lives with you
now and later will be in you."

~ John 14:16-17 NLT

358

The LORD will not forsake you nor
destroy you, nor forget the covenant
of your fathers which He swore to them.

~ Deuteronomy 4:31 NKJV

359

The LORD is good; His mercy
is everlasting, and His truth
endures to all generations.

~ Psalm 100:5 NKJV

360

The LORD your God is the God of gods
and Lord of lords. He is the great God,
the mighty and awesome God, who shows
no partiality and cannot be bribed.

~ Deuteronomy 10:17 NLT

361

His anger lasts only a moment, but His favor
lasts a lifetime! Weeping may last through
the night, but joy comes with the morning.

~ Psalm 30:5 NLT

The Lord is good

362

You are the glory of their strength,
and in Your favor our horn is exalted.

~ *Psalm 89:17 NKJV*

363

What is man that You are mindful of him,
and the son of man that You care for him?
Yet You have made him a little lower than
the heavenly beings and crowned him
with glory and honor.

~ *Psalm 8:4-5 ESV*

364

Because Your steadfast love is better
than life, my lips will praise You.

~ *Psalm 63:3* ESV

365

I will exalt You, my God the King;
I will praise Your name for ever and ever.
Every day I will praise You and extol Your
name for ever and ever.

~ *Psalm 145:1-2* NIV